NORMAL PUBLIC LIBRARY
206 W. COLLEGE AVE.
NORMAL, IL 61761

DEMCO

NATIONAL GEOGRAPHIC CHANNEL

GREAT MIGRATIONS

Butterflies

Laura Marsh

NATIONAL
GEOGRAPHIC

Washington, D.C.

For Aunt Jodie
— L.F.M.

Paperback ISBN: 978-1-4263-0739-3
Library binding ISBN: 978-1-4263-0740-9

Printed in China
10/RRDS/1

Abbreviation Key: GET = Getty Images; IS = iStockphoto.com; NGS = NationalGeographicStock.com; NGT = National Geographic Television; SS = Shutterstock.com

Cover, Medford Taylor/NGS; 1, Patricio Robles Gil/Minden Pictures/NGS; 2 (center), James P. Blair/NGS; 4 (bottom), NGT; 5 (bottom), NGT; 5 (top), John Eastcott & Yva Momatiuk/NGS; 6, Darlyne A. Murawski/NGS; 10–11 (center), Annie Griffiths/NGS; 12, Annie Griffiths/NGS; 12–13 (top), Patricio Robles Gil/Minden Pictures/ NGS; 14–15 (center), Digital Vision/GET; 14 (center right), M. Dykstra/SS; 15 (top right), Ambient Ideas/SS; 16–17 (center), James L. Amos/NGS; 20 (center), Annie Griffiths/NGS; 21 (top left), NGT; 22 (top right), Xavi Heredia/ NGS; 22 (right center), Eran Mahalu/IS; 22 (bottom right), Buck Lovell/NGS; 23 (center), Paul Sutherland/NGS; 24 (left), Ivanastar/IS; 24 (right), Daniel Loretto/IS; 25 (left), Derek Croucher/Photographer's Choice/GET; 25 (right), Comstock/GET; 27 (top), Larry Minden/Minden Pictures/NGS;27 (left center), Bianca Lavies/NGS; 28 (center), Tom Till/Photographer's Choice/GET; 28, M. Dykstra/SS; 29 (bottom center), NGT; 29, Ambient Ideas/SS; 30 (center), Paul Zahl/NGS; 31 (center), NGT; 32 (top), Paul Zahl/NGS; 32 (bottom), George Grall/NGS; 33 (bottom left), George Grall/NGS; 34–35 (center), Cathy Keifer/SS; 36 (center), Fotosearch; 37 (center), Phil Schermeister/ NGS; 37 (bottom right), ; 38 (top right), NGT; 38 (bottom center), George Grall/NGS; 38 (right center), Eric Bean/ The Image Bank/GET; 38 (bottom left), NGT; 38 (bottom right), Bianca Lavies/NGS; 38 (top left), George Grall/ NGS; 39 (top left), George Grall/NGS; 39 (top right), NGT; 39 (left center), NHY59/IS; 39 (right center), Bianca Lavies/NGS; 39 (bottom center), James P. Blair/NGS; 40–41 (UP CTR), Mattias Klum/NGS; 41 (bottom center), Patricio Robles Gil/NGS; 42–43, Jamie Dertz/NGS; 44 (bottom right), Donna Coleman/IS; 45 (center), Fotosearch; 46 (top right), Biance Lavies/NGS; 46 (left center), April Moore/NGS; 46 (right center), Phil Schermeister/NGS; 46 (bottom left), Paul Sutherland/NGS; 46 (bottom right), NGT; 47 (top right), NGT; 47 (top right), Andy Dean/ IS; 47 (left center), Ambient Images/SS; 47 (right center), Eric Bean/The Image Bank/GET; 47 (bottom left), Jamie Dertz/NGS; 47 (bottom right), Patricio Robles Gil/Minden Pictures/NGS; 47, Digital Vision/GET

Table of Contents

On the Move

When animals travel from one region or habitat to another, it is called migration. Animals migrate in search of food or a mate. Migration helps animals survive on Earth.

Many animals migrate. The monarch butterfly is one of them.

monarchs

wildebeest

red crabs

Wing Words

MIGRATION: Moving from one region or habitat to another for food or a mate

MATE: Either a male or female in a pair. Most animals need a mate to have babies.

Amazing Monarchs

What insect is black and orange and flies the farthest of any on Earth?

You guessed it, a monarch butterfly!

Monarch butterflies migrate 2,000 to 3,000 miles. They travel to the forests of Mexico from the United States and Canada—and back—every year.

Since butterflies are so small, a mile is much farther for them than for people. A butterfly's 2,800-mile trip is like a person traveling 275,000 miles. That's like walking around Earth 11 times!

Mighty Big Trip

Rocky Mountains

Western
Migration

Eastern
Migration

Mexico

weird but true Monarch caterpillars get oxygen through holes in the sides of their bodies.

Canada

United
States

Two Monarch Populations

The western population migrates along the Pacific coast of the United States. The eastern population migrates east of the Rocky Mountains in the United States and Canada all the way to Mexico. This book is about the eastern population.

It is winter.
In the Oyamel
(Oh-ya-mehl)
forests of Mexico,
clusters of butterflies
make the trees look
orange. There are
so many butterflies,
they could cover
11 football fields!
Here the monarchs
rest and wait for
spring.

weird
but
true

Antennae give
butterflies a
sense of smell.

In the spring, swarms of newly awakened monarchs cover the trees and fly through the air. Millions of monarchs are ready to leave Mexico.

Need to Lead

The female monarchs lead the butterflies north from Mexico.

Their parents cannot guide them. They died soon after the eggs were laid. How do these butterflies know where to go?

The monarchs know where to go by instinct. Sunlight signals them to migrate. Scientists believe that sunlight also helps guide them.

It Takes the Whole Family

Each year, the monarchs' migration takes several generations. Three or four generations complete the trip north. But only one generation makes the return trip south.

That means that if you started the journey, your great, great grandchildren would finish it.

How does this work?

Wing Word

GENERATION: Time it takes for a living thing to grow up and reproduce

The first three or four generations live two to six weeks as adult butterflies. During the spring, the first generation hatches in the south. They fly north as far as they can. Then they lay eggs and later die.

The second generation continues the journey, lays eggs, and dies. The third and sometimes fourth generations hatch through the spring and summer. They finish the journey north.

Adults appear to have four legs, but they really have six. Their two front legs are small. They are curled up and hard to see.

Canada

United States

4th

3rd

2nd

Mexico

1st

Oyamel
Forests

19

At the end of the summer, a special super generation hatches. These butterflies live six to nine months, much longer than the generations before it.

In the fall when it gets colder in the north, the monarchs fly south. They fly all the way back to the Oyamel forests in Mexico. This takes about two months. It is a long and dangerous journey.

Danger!

Predators

Migrating butterflies make a delicious snack for many predators. To keep enemies away, monarchs have built-in protection.

praying mantis

fire ants

oriole

Wing Words

PREDATOR: An animal that eats other animals

TOXIN: A poison from a living thing

Monarch predators include spiders, black-eared mice, praying mantises, fire ants, and birds such as orioles and grosbeaks.

Milkweed has toxins in it. When monarch caterpillars eat milkweed, it makes their skin poisonous. It even tastes bad. This keeps predators away.

MILKWEED: A flowering plant with milky juice

Wing Word

But some predators can withstand the toxins or feed on monarchs without eating their skin.

23

Cold Temperatures

Monarchs need warm temperatures to fly. When temperatures get too low, monarchs will die.

Wind and Rain

Butterflies flock to the trees for shelter during high winds and rain. They cannot fly during bad weather.

How Deadly?

A rainstorm with low temperatures killed as many as 250 million monarchs in Mexico in 2002. An estimated 80 percent of the butterflies died at one of the mountain sanctuaries.

Tiring Travel

Did you know that migrating monarchs can fly up to 30 miles per hour? That's about three times faster than we can run.

Monarchs usually fly 50-100 miles a day when they are migrating. But the farthest recorded monarch travel is 265 miles in one day. Whew! That's tiring just to think about.

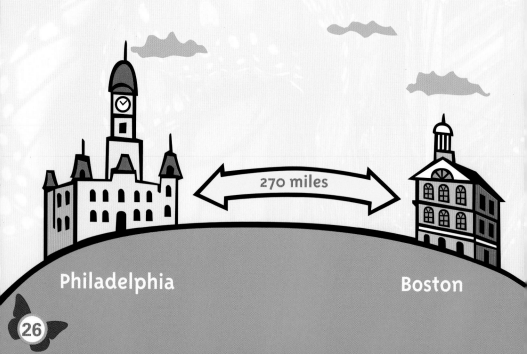

270 miles

Philadelphia

Boston

tag

Monarch Tracking

Scientists learn about monarchs by tracking them. Small tags are put on monarchs' wings. If a tagged butterfly is caught, the tag number, date, and place are entered into a website. Then scientists know how many miles the butterfly flew. They also know how long it took. You can help tag monarchs, too. To find out more, go to www.monarchwatch.org.

In the winter, monarchs rest from their long journey. They wake in the spring, lay their eggs, and die soon after.

When the eggs hatch, a new first generation begins again. This generation will start the journey north.

From Egg to Butterfly

There are four stages in a butterfly's life.

1 Egg

A mother butterfly places her eggs on a milkweed leaf. A tiny butterfly egg is the size of a pinhead. This stage lasts 4 days.

Hard Working Mamas!

A female carries up to 400 eggs. She flies from leaf to leaf. On each leaf she places only one or two eggs. That's a lot of work!

weird but true

A monarch caterpillar eats its eggshell before it starts eating milkweed.

② Caterpillar

A tiny caterpillar hatches from the egg. It eats milkweed all day long. In two weeks it grows from less than a quarter inch to two inches long.

❸ Chrysalis

A caterpillar creates a hard, protective coating around itself called a chrysalis. From outside, it appears that nothing is happening. But inside, the caterpillar is transforming into a butterfly. This stage lasts about ten days.

Wing Word

CHRYSALIS: An insect between larva and adult stage in a hardened case or cocoon

After 10-12 days, the chrysalis becomes clear and cracks open.

The butterfly comes out head first.

Its wings are small and crumpled.

④ **Butterfly**

When the chrysalis opens, a butterfly is born!

The monarch pumps liquid through the veins in its wings to enlarge them.

The butterfly's veins stiffen. About one hour after it comes out of the chrysalis, the monarch is ready to fly.

35

Munching Monarchs

When monarchs are in the caterpillar stage, they only eat milkweed plants. And they eat a lot.

Adult monarchs eat the sweet nectar from many different flowering plants, including milkweed. The nectar gives the butterflies energy to fly.

Wing Word

NECTAR: Sweet plant juice eaten by insects

10 Cool Things About Monarchs

1 They can flap their wings up to 2,000 times a minute.

2 Their green chrysalis looks as if it's beaded with gold.

3 An adult sucks nectar and water through its straw-like tongue, called a proboscis.

4 Their bright colors warn predators they are poisonous.

5 When caterpillars become too large for their skin, they shed it and grow new skin.

6

Predators kill 15 percent of the monarchs in Mexico every year.

7

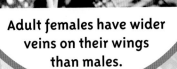

MALE FEMALE

Adult females have wider veins on their wings than males.

8

Though strong enough to fly 2,000 miles, a butterfly weighs less than a paper clip.

9

A newly hatched butterfly has to wait for its wings to stiffen before it can fly away.

10

Scientists think monarchs have been migrating for thousands of years.

At Risk

Humans love monarchs, but they can harm them by accident.

Wing Word

HABITAT: The place or environment where a plant or animal naturally lives

In the forests of Mexico, many trees where they live have been cut down. This is called deforestation. Monarchs need trees for protection against wind and rain. Deforestation is a big problem for monarch butterflies.

Wing Word

DEFORESTATION: Cutting down forests of trees

Monarchs are also losing their milkweed. People use chemicals to stop it from growing. They see milkweed as a harmful weed.

Monarch butterflies can't live without milkweed or the forests of Mexico. Humans and monarchs need to learn to share the Earth.

Caterpillars have six pairs of tiny eyes, but they don't see well.

What You Can Do

There are many ways to help monarchs. Tagging butterflies is one way.

You can also plant a butterfly garden. This special garden gives monarchs a place to rest, feed, and lay eggs so that they can continue on their amazing journey.

To find out more about monarch butterflies, check out these groups that help them:

National Geographic
http://animals.nationalgeographic.com/animals/bugs/monarch-butterfly.html

World Wildlife Fund
http://www.worldwildlife.org/species/finder/monarchbutter-flies/monarchbutterflies.html

Journey North
http://www.learner.org/jnorth/monarch/index.html

Glossary

MIGRATION: Moving from one region or habitat to another for food or a mate

GENERATION: The time it takes for a living thing to grow up and reproduce

PREDATOR: An animal that eats other animals

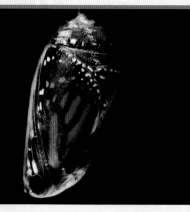

CHRYSALIS: An insect between larva and adult stage in a hardened case or cocoon

46

NECTAR: A sweet plant juice eaten by monarchs and other insects

MATE: Either a male or female in a pair. Most animals need a mate to have babies.

INSTINCT: Behavior that animals are born knowing how to do

TOXIN: A poison from a living thing

MILKWEED: A flowering plant with milky juice

HABITAT: The place or environment where a plant or animal naturally lives

DEFORESTATION: Cutting down forests of trees

Index